COUNSELS OF LIGHT AND LOVE

Counsels
of
Light and Love

ST. JOHN OF THE CROSS

Introduction by Thomas Merton

Adapted from THE COMPLETE WORKS OF
ST JOHN OF THE CROSS *by E. Allison Peers*

Paulist Press
New York, N.Y./Ramsey, N.J.

Library of Congress
Catalog Card Number: 78-64359
ISBN: 0-8091-2069-0

First published in the United States of America in 1978 by
Paulist Press
Editorial Office: 1865 Broadway, New York, N.Y. 10023
Business Office: 545 Island Road, Ramsey, N.J. 07446
Printed and bound in
theUnited States of America

CONTENTS

TO
THE SPIRIT OF LOVE
DIVINE COUNSELLOR
OF THE TRANSLUCENT SOUL
OF SAINT JOHN OF THE CROSS

FOREWORD

The intention in offering the Cautelas and Points of Light and Love in a convenient pocketsize manual is that they may find their way into the hands and hearts, not only of the sons and daughters of St. John, but also that vast army of religious and thinking lay-folk who are turning their eyes to the Mystical Mount of Carmel, eager to discover the ascending paths whereby they may attain to the "peaceful rest of the spirit," and the intimacy of Divine Love.

Mine are the Heavens and mine is the earth;
mine are the people, - - -
the righteous are mine and mine are the sinners;
the Angels are mine . . . and the Mother of God,
and all things are mine; - - -
and God Himself is mine and for me, - - -
for Christ is mine and all for me.
What then dost thou ask for and seek, my soul?
Thine is all this, and it is all for thee.

St. John: Prayer of An Enamored Soul.

INTRODUCTION

Light in Darkness—
The Ascetic Doctrine of
St. John of the Cross

IN understanding the sanctity and doctrine of St. John of the Cross, the first thing we must do is to see them in the clear perspectives of the New Testament, the Sermon on the Mount, the profound discourses in the Gospel of St. John, and particularly the mystery of the Passion and the Resurrection of the Son of God. In this way, we will be preserved from the danger of giving the writings of the Carmelite Doctor a kind of stoical bias which makes his austerity seem pointlessly inhuman, and which, instead of opening our hearts to divine grace closes them in upon themselves in fanatical rigidity.

There are plenty of "hard sayings" in St. John of the Cross, just as there were hard sayings in the Gospel. Our Lord said that we must "hate our Father and Mother . . . and even our own life." But we know that the hard sayings in the Gospel need to be properly qualified and understood. The command to "hate" Father and Mother, which at times seems so scandalous, does not interfere with the commandment to love and revere them. It is simply a strong statement of the hierarchy of value for the Christian—in which the salvation of his own soul comes before everything else, and in which, *if there arises a choice* between the love of parents and the love of truth, or the love of one's own life and fidelity to the word of God, then one's natural love must be sacrificed.

1

This same principle will serve to explain many of the seemingly harsh and extreme statements of St. John of the Cross. His whole asceticism is basically a question of choice, of preference. And we cannot understand what he is talking about if we do not see what the choice really is. On the one hand, the love and the will of God: on the other, the love and the gratification of self. But what do these alternatives mean *in practice*? If we merely take them in the abstract, then the asceticism of St. John of the Cross becomes something mechanical, cold, soulless and inhuman: a kind of mathematical exclusion of all spontaneity in favor of dreary and rigid self-punishment. But if we see what he is talking about in the concrete, it is quite a different matter. For on the one hand, we have the confused, dissipated, and unruly urges of our undisciplined desire, which draw us into a state of blindness, weariness, distraction and exile from God. On the other hand there are the very real and very urgent inspirations of the Holy Spirit of Divine Wisdom, that "loving, tranquil, lonely and peaceful sweet inebriator of the spirit. Hereby the soul feels itself to be gently and tenderly wounded and ravished, knowing not by whom, nor whence, nor how" (*Living Flame of Love*, iii, 38 Vol III p. 181). One who does not genuinely experience in himself the reality of these two alternatives cannot fully appreciate the ascetic teaching of St. John of the Cross. However, even those who are not themselves mystics can profit by reading his works, if only they remember to see them in perspective.

When St. John of the Cross says, for instance, that we must treat our companions in the monastery as if they were not there, he can be tragically misunderstood by anyone who does not know precisely what the saint is

2

aiming at. He certainly does not mean that we should simply stifle our spontaneous love and live like creatures without sensibility or affection. This would, in fact, be a sin not only against charity but even against temperance (Insensibility is a sin against temperance, says St. Thomas: II II Q. 142a. 1). On the contrary, St. John *presumes* a very special situation: a community of contemplatives in which all have a definite call to "enjoy" the much higher and more spiritual form of love that we have suggested above. This secret, silent, contemplative union with God does not in fact exclude fraternal union but on the contrary it contains it within itself. Those who live the contemplative life on this level, are all the more closely united with one another in proportion as they grow in spiritual union with God. Therefore St. John of the Cross is certainly very wise in warning them against the temptation to become too preoccupied with one another on a more exterior, more conventional level, which would in fact keep them from growing in true delicacy of love. Experience in the contemplative life shows us that spiritual confusion awaits those who yield to foolish and sentimental impulse under the guise of charity, and allow themselves to lose their first fruits of prayer in an absurdly useless preoccupation with the lives of those around them. They become nothing else but sentimental busybodies, interfering with the order of the community, the peace of their companions, and the secret action of the Holy Spirit. Sometimes this false charity proceeds from a hidden sensuality, and in other cases it is an expression of latent activism, an attempt to escape from the interior solitude of the contemplative with the deprivations it implies. Such temptations are quite natural, of course:

3

but a spirituality that is basically active and extraverted will not help one to meet the problem in a contemplative way. St. John of the Cross firmly and resolutely sticks to his viewpoint. His way may seem drastic, but it can lead one to the interior detachment and tranquility without which a full contemplative life is impossible.

Seen in this light, the *Cautions*, addressed to the community of nuns which the saint directed at Beas in Andalusia, is likely to be interpreted more wisely. The same things would not be said in the same way either to the people in the world, or to religious living the active life. Incidentally, notice the obvious human tenderness with which St. John of the Cross writes in his letters to these nuns. It is well known that he had a special preference for this community (headed by the saintly Anne of Jesus) and he made no effort to disguise the fact that the nuns were a great consolation to him. But his love was simple and supernatural. It was not based on merely superficial considerations, but on a deep sharing of ideals and love "in the Spirit." In any case, we can see that the saint practiced what he preached and was able at the same time to love these souls who had been confided to his direction by the Lord, and to be perfectly detached in his love for them. This "reconciliation of opposites" is the mark of true sanctity. Needless to add, it gives the soul of the saint a perfectly Christlike character, for every page of the Gospel shows us, in Christ Our Lord, a supreme harmony between well-ordered human feelings and the demands of a divine nature and personality.

All the doctrine of St. John of the Cross is aimed at this ideal balance of the human and the divine: a balance that is to be attained, however, not on a humanistic level, but "in the Spirit." Now if our human nature is to be brought under the complete and exclusive control of the Spirit of Light, then there is only one way: to follow Christ in His passion and to rise with Him from the dead. The "passion" in our life is our crucifixion by asceticism and by passive purification, especially by mystical trials. Our resurrection is the joy and the peace of contemplative prayer, and union with the Divine Spouse in mystical love.

Just as we can never separate asceticism from mysticism, so in St. John of the Cross we find darkness and light, suffering and joy, sacrifice and love united together so closely that they seem at times to be identified. It is not so much that we come through darkness to light, as that the darkness itself is light.

> Never was fount so clear, undimmed and bright;
> From it alone, I know, proceeds all light,
>   Although 'tis night.

Hence the essential simplicity of his teaching: enters into the night and you will be enlightened. "Night" means the "darkening" of all our natural desires, our natural understanding, our human way of loving; but this darkening brings with it an enlightenment. The greater our sacrifice, the deeper the night into which we plunge, the more promptly and more completely will we be enlightened. But the point to be carefully remembered is that we are *not enlightened by our own efforts, our own love, our own sacrifice*. These, on the contrary, are darkness. Even our highest spiritual abilities are darkness in the sight of God. All must be "darkened" that is to say, forgotten, in order that God Himself may become the light of our soul. The "darkness" which St. John teaches is not a pure negation. Rather it is the removal and extinguishing of a lesser light in order that pure light may shine in its place. It is like putting out a candle which is no longer of any use in the full light of day. The problem, of course, is that we *do not see* the spiritual daylight of God's presence all around us, we see only the candlelight of our own desires and judgments. This is of course familiar doctrine, common to all ascetic theologians. But one special point is emphasized by St. John of the Cross. He would extinguish not only the "light" of sensual and inordinate desires, but even certain desires, judgments and illuminations which appear to be good and holy. Indeed, he proceeds by the "darkening" even of those good and helpful notions of God, those lights and consolations of prayer which have an important positive part to play in the beginnings of the spiritual life. But as we go on, if we become attached to these thoughts, ideas and images of God, and remain concerned with ourselves and our spiritual progress, we will not be able to "see" the purer and more spiritual light of God Himself. Hence, as the saint says:

It is clear that, in order perfectly to attain to union in this life through grace and through love, a soul must be in darkness with respect to all that can enter through the eye, and to all that can be received through the ear, and can be imagined with the fancy, and understood with the heart, which here signifies the soul. And thus a soul is greatly impeded from reaching this high estate of union with God when it clings to any understanding or feeling or imagination or appearance or will or manner of its own, or to any other act or to anything of its own, and cannot detach and strip itself of all these. For, as we say, the goal which it seeks is beyond all this, yea, beyond even the highest thing that can be known or experienced; and thus a soul must pass beyond everything to unknowing. (Ascent of Mount Carmel, II IV, Vol. i, p. 76)

This enables us to understand the peculiar emphasis in the Sayings upon quietness, silence, solitude, and the "absence of business and bustle" in the interior life.

> Since God is inaccessible, do not concern yourself with how much your faculties can comprehend and your senses can perceive or you will be satisfied with less and your soul will lose the swiftness that is necessary for one who wants to attain Him.

> On the road to life there is very little bustle and business, and it requires mortification of the will rather than much knowledge. He who encumbers himself least with things and pleasures will go farthest along the road.

> The soul that does not shake off anxiety and does not quench desire in its journey toward God is like a man who drags a cart uphill.

Finally, this gives us an insight into the reason why St. John of the Cross tells his penitents to welcome darkness and spiritual trials as a great good, and assures them that when they are without consolation and light in prayer, and are fully aware of their own poverty, God is probably closer to them than ever before. Of course, this is not a universal principle for all, but it applies to those who are called to the way of contemplative prayer.

If we read the saint carefully, and take care to weigh every word, we will see that he is preaching a doctrine of pure liberty which is the very heart of the New Testament. He wants us to be free. He wants to liberate

7

us not only from the captivity of passion and egoism, but even from the more subtle tyranny of spiritual ambition, and preoccupation with methods of prayer and systems for making progress. But of course, one must first be *called* to this contemplative prayer. Here is what he says:

> Wherefore in this state the soul must never have meditation imposed upon it, nor must it perform any acts, nor strive after sweetness of fervor; for this would be to set an obstacle in the way of the principal agent, who . . . is God. For God secretly and quietly infuses into the soul loving knowledge and wisdom without any intervention of specific acts, although he sometimes produces them in the soul for some length of time. And the soul has then to walk in loving awareness of God, without performing specific acts, but conducting itself as we have said passively, and having no diligence of its own, but possessing this pure, simple and loving awareness, as one that opens his eyes with an awareness of love. (*Living Flame of Love* iii, ew, Vol. iii, p. 77)

Most of *the maxims and teachings collected here point to this special kind of interior peace, detachment and emptiness. St. John of the Cross strives to liberate the soul from trivial and exterior concerns, and even from lesser, more busy forms of active asceticism, in order that it may rest in detached unconcern, and yield in all simplicity to the secret action of God.* The great thing is to be delivered from useless desires, desires which though they appear to be very profitable and efficacious, in reality lead us off the right road because they emphasize our own action more than the action of grace. This is St. John's main concern: that contemplatives should not waste their time and their efforts in doing work that only has to be undone by God and done over again, if they are to come to union with Him.

> It is very needful, my daughters, to be able to withdraw the spirit from the devil and from sensuality, for otherwise without knowing it we shall find ourselves completely failing to make progress and very far removed from the virtues of Christ, and afterwards we shall awaken and find our work and labour inside out. Thinking that our lamp was burning, we shall find it apparently extinguished, for when we blew it, and thought thereby to fan its flame, we may rather have put it out. (Letter vi, to the Nuns of Beas)

St. John was no quietist. On the contrary few saints make more insistent demands for the right kind of work: but this work is all interior. It consists in love and suffering, not in external projects that make much noise and raise a lot of dust but, in the end, leave us no further advanced than we were before. The same letter we have just quoted insists, a few lines further down: "It is impossible to continue to make progress save by working and suffering with all virtue, *and being completely enwrapped in silence*."

The last phrase is what is most important, and most characteristic of St. John of the Cross. It is the key to his asceticism of light in darkness, which seeks in all things to bring the soul into the *interior depths* where love is invisible, and to rescue it from the triviality of the obvious and showy forms of spiritual life which are good only for those who remain on the surface.

Any one of the maxims of St. John of the Cross is an inexhaustible mine of spiritual truth for the reader who really, sincerely and humbly seeks to renounce himself

9

and abandon himself, in faith, to the mercy of God.

The ascetic teaching of St. John of the Cross is part and parcel of his mysticism and cannot be separated from it. That is why *the poems in this volume happily complete the aphorisms and cautions, and incite the reader to go on to the saint's great mystical treatises which are nothing but commentaries on his poems.* The remarkable beauty of his poems *shows that his asceticism, far from destroying his creative genius, had liberated and transformed it by dedicating it to God.*

Thomas Merton
Abbey of Gethsemane
Trappist, Kentucky

CAUTIONS

Introduction

NONE of St. John of the Cross's admirers would contend that his minor prose writings, of which the *Cautions* is the first in order, have anything approaching the same value as the four great treatises by which he is chiefly remembered. They are but crumbs which have fallen from his table, and yet so well-furnished is that table and so genuine are they—so completely unified, in other words, is his teaching—that even those who are familiar with the great ascetico-mystical commentaries would deeply regret their loss.

The gift of St. John of the Cross for combining synthetic with analytic writing gives his minor prose works a character quite their own. He talked and wrote easily and fluently, it is true; but he evidently had a liking for condensed, maxim-like methods of expression: it will be remembered that St. Teresa dubbed him her "little Seneca." Probably a large proportion of these works have disappeared, for most of them were addressed to individuals—penitents of the author—and would naturally suffer the same fate as private letters. Some of the more impersonal, which are of fairly general application to those who lead the religious life, have escaped destruction, and one of the chief of these is that known briefly as *Cautions*.

More exactly, its title is "Cautions which any who would be a true religious and would quickly attain to perfection must needs bear ever in mind." It has nine sections, in which the religious is warned against man's three most fearful and deadly enemies—the world, the devil and the flesh. Being brief, they can easily be learned by heart and repeated in moments of leisure, perplexity or temptation. The words in the title "attain to perfection" should be carefully noticed. Even in a short and purely ascetic treatise, the Saint has always in mind the goal of union with God.

The *Cautions* was one of the first of the Saint's writings to be composed when he retired to El Calvario and became regular confessor to the Discalced Carmelite nuns of Beas. In her depositions for the Beatification process made at Beas in 1618, Ana de Jesús, one of the first nuns of that convent and for some time the Saint's penitent, deposed that "when he went away (from Beas), he left the nuns some cautions concerning the enemies of the soul and a few sentences for each one; and this witness has all those which he left her, with as many more as she could get, and she considers them to be of great value for her consolation." Again, early in the seventeenth century, the diligent P. Alonso de la Madre de Dios wrote at the end of a description of the Saint's writings:

> Other short spiritual treatises he composed, which have not yet been printed; among these, I have one containing nine cautions with which we may challenge the three enemies of the soul. These he wrote at the request of the Discalced nuns of Beas.

There are other early testimonies to the authenticity of this opuscule, though, with certain others, it passed unmentioned by many witnesses who mentioned the *Ascent*, the *Dark Night*, the *Canticle* and the *Living Flame*.

Few early copies of the *Cautions* have survived: so slight a document was only too easily lost, though a multitude of copies of it must have been made, in view

12

of that same brevity and the nature of its argument. It may be doubted if there were any Discalced friars and nuns who seriously aimed at spiritual progress and had not at sometime handled a copy of this little treatise. But, as the printed editions of the Saint's works multiplied, the necessity for these copies grew less and in mid-eighteenth century P. Andrés discovered only a few, and those chiefly in Andalusia. In them he found a considerable number of textual variants, which he attributes partly to revisions by St. John of the Cross himself, since, as he says, not all of them can very well be copyists' errors and there was less scope for correction in that type of treatise. This is quite possible, as we know that the Saint revised the brief "Mount of Perfection" as well as the extensive *Spiritual Canticle* and *Living Flame*. Still, into generations of copies made at second, third or fourth hand, it is not surprising if there crept innumerable errors of all kinds and it is impossible to do more than speculate on their origin and nature.

The *Cautions* was not included in the *editio princeps* of 1618, nor, although he certainly knew it and mentioned it in his *History* (Bk. IV, chap. viii), did Fray Jerónimo de San José publish it in his edition of 1630. It first appeared in a Latin translation of St. John of the Cross's works which was published at Cologne in 1639. [The first Spanish edition seems to have been published at Gerona, by P. Jerónimo de la Asunción, in 1650.] In 1667, another edition was published by P. Esteban de San José together with some of the *Maxims*. The first collected Spanish edition in which it appeared was that of Barcelona, 1693; here it bore the title "Instruction and Caution which any man who would be a true religious and would quickly attain to great perfection must ever bear in mind."

Of the few early copies of the opuscule which are still extent, the best is certainly MS. 6,296, which comes down to us from P. Andrés de la Encarnación and which we follow in the edition as did P. Gerardo also in that of 1912.

CAUTIONS

which must be kept in mind by all
who would become true religious
and attain perfection
Addressed to the Carmelite Nuns of Beas

THE following instructions must be practiced by any religious who desires to attain quickly that holy recollection, silence, spiritual detachment and poverty of spirit in which the peaceful refreshment of the Holy Spirit is enjoyed, and by means of which the soul attains to union with God, and frees itself from the hindrances which come from all the creatures of this world, and defends itself from the wiles and deceits of the devil, and is freed from itself.

2. With habitual care he will very quickly come to great perfection, gaining all the virtues and attaining holy peace. No further labor or other kind of exercise is necessary except those which his state calls for.

3. It is necessary to see that the evils which the soul receives come from the enemies mentioned above; the world, the devil, and the flesh. The world is the least difficult; the devil is the hardest to understand. The flesh is the most tenacious of all and its assaults continue for as long as the old man exists.

4. In order to conquer any one of these three, it is necessary to conquer all three of them; for, if one is weakened, the other two are weakened. When all three are conquered, no more war remains in the soul.

Against the World

5. In order to free yourself perfectly from the evil which the world can do, you should use three cautions.

First Caution

6. The first caution is that you should have equal love and equal detachment for all persons, whether they are relatives or not; you must withdraw your heart from all equally. More so, indeed, in some ways, from your relatives, in case flesh and blood come alive with the natural love which is always alive among relatives and must be mortified for the sake of spiritual perfection. Hold them all as strangers to you; in this way you serve them better than by setting upon them the affection which you owe God. Do not love one person more than another or you will go astray, for he whom God loves best is worthy to be loved best; and you do not know who it is that God loves best. But if you are equally detached from them all, as is proper for you for holy recollection, you will free yourself from going astray regarding the greater or lesser degree of love due to each. Do not think of them at all, whether good or ill; flee from them insofar as you can. And, if you do not observe this, you have not learned to be a religious. You will not be able to attain holy recollection, nor free yourself from the imperfections that come as a result of this. If in this manner you desire to allow yourself a certain license, the devil will deceive you in one way or another, or you will deceive yourself, under some color of good or evil. In following this advice lies security, for in no other way can you free yourself from the imperfections and evils which the soul receives from creatures.

Second Caution

7. The second caution against the world is with respect to temporal good things. If you want to truly free yourself from this kind of evil and moderate the excesses of your appetite, it is necessary to abhor all kinds of possessions and to have no concern for them, not for food, clothing, nor any created thing, nor for the future. Your concern must be directed to something higher, that is to seeking the kingdom of God, to not fail God; and the rest, as His majesty says, will be added to us. For He that cares for the beasts will not forget you. In this way you will attain silence and peace in the senses.

Third Caution

8. The third caution is very necessary if you are to learn to guard yourself in the convent from all evil regarding the other religious. Many, through not observing it, have not only lost the peace and blessing of their souls, but have fallen, and continue to fall into many evils and sins. This caution is that you should diligently keep yourself from setting your thoughts upon what happens in the community, and still more, from speaking of it; nor should you think of what may concern, or may have concerned, some other religious in particular. You should not speak of his character, or of his manner of life, or of any of his business, however grave, either under the pretext of zeal or the desire to remedy matters, except to the person to whom it is right and at the proper time. Nor should you ever be shocked or marvel at anything that you see or hear, but rather should strive to keep your soul in forgetfulness of it all.

9. For if you do consider any of these matters, even if

you live among angels, many things will seem wrong, since you will not understand the substance of them. Take as an example Lot's wife: because she was troubled at the destruction of the Sodomites, she looked backward to see what was happening; and was punished by God, who turned her into a statue of salt. By this you should understand that even if you live among devils, God wills you to live among them in such a way that you do not look back in your thoughts at their business, but that you abandon them wholly, striving to keep your soul pure and sincere with God, undisturbed by thoughts of one thing or another. You may take it for granted that convents and communities will never be without some occasion of stumbling, since devils who strive to overthrow the saints are never lacking, and God permits this in order to exercise and prove them. And if you do not keep yourself, as has been said, as if you were not in the house, you can never be a religious, no matter what you do, nor attain holy detachment and recollection, nor free yourself from the inherent evils. For, if you do not do this, however good may be your purpose and however great your zeal, the devil will entrap you in one place or another, for you are already securely entrapped when you permit your soul to be distracted in any of these ways. Remember what the apostle Saint James says: "If any man thinks himself to be religious, bridling not his tongue, this man's religion is vain." This is to be understood no less of inner speech than of outer.

Against the Devil

10. These three cautions should be used by whoever aspires to perfection, in order that he may free himself

from the devil, his second enemy. For this reason it is necessary to see that among the many wiles used by the devil to deceive spiritual persons, the most common is that of deceiving them under the appearance of what is good, not under the appearance of what is evil. For he knows that if they recognize evil they will not touch it. Therefore, you must always have misgivings concerning that which seems good when it is not commanded to you by obedience. Security and success in this matter come from taking proper counsel in it.

First Caution

11. Let the first caution then be that except when you are commanded by obligation you should be moved to nothing; however good and full of charity it may seem, whether it be for yourself or anyone in or out of the house, unless ordered by obedience. In observing this you will gain merit and security. Avoid attachment and you will flee from the devil and from evils you do not know, but of which God shall call for an account of you in His time. If you do not observe this caution both in little things and in great, however successful you seem to be, you cannot fail to be deceived by the devil either to a small or to a great degree. Even if you do no worse than fail to be ruled in all things by obedience, you have strayed and are to be blamed. God prefers obedience to sacrifice, and the actions of a religious are not his own but belong to obedience and if you withdraw them from obedience, you will have to count them as lost.

Second Caution

12. Let the second caution be that you never consider your superior as less than if he were God, no

matter who the superior may be, for to you he stands in the place of God. Realize that the devil, the enemy of humility, meddles greatly in this. If you consider your superior in this way, you gain and profit greatly; if otherwise, your loss and harm are great. Therefore be vigilant in keeping yourself from considering his character, ways, habits or any of his other characteristics or else you will do yourself the harm of exchanging Divine obedience for human, by being moved or unmoved only by the visible characteristics of your superior instead of by the invisible God Whom you serve in his person. Your obedience will be vain, or more unfruitful, if you take offense at any unpleasing characteristic in your superior, or rejoice because you find him good and pleasant. For I tell you, the devil has ruined the perfection of a great many religious by causing them to consider these characteristics; their obedience is of very little worth in the eyes of God, because they have considered these things and have not paid sole respect to obedience. Unless you strive until you become indifferent in your feelings whether this one or that is your superior, you can in no way become a spiritual person nor keep your vows well.

Third Caution

13. The third caution aimed directly against the devil is that you strive always to humble your heart in word and in deed, rejoicing at the good of others as at your own and desiring that others be preferred to yourself in all things and this with all your heart. In this way you will overcome evil with good, cast the devil far from yourself and have joy of heart. Strive to practice this most with respect to those least attractive to you. And

know that unless you practice this, you shall not attain true charity nor make progress in it. And love always to be taught by all men rather than desiring to teach him who is least of all.

Against the Flesh

14. Three further cautions should be observed by anyone who desires to conquer himself and his sensual nature, which is his third enemy.

First Caution

15. The first caution is that you should understand that you have come to the convent only that all may form and try you. Thus, in order to free yourself from the imperfections and disturbances that may arise from the temperaments and habits of the religious and in order to take advantage from every happening, you must think of everyone in the convent as workmen who are to try you, as in truth they are. For some have to form you by word, others by deed and others by their thoughts against you. You may be subject to them in all things, even as an image is subject to the one who forms it, to the one who paints it and to the one who gilds it. If you do not observe this, you will not be able to overcome your sensual nature and your feelings, nor shall you be able to conduct yourself well in the convent with the religious, nor attain holy peace, nor free yourself from many evils and occasions of stumbling.

Second Caution

16. The second caution is that you should never fail to perform any good work, if it is fitting that they be

done in the service of Our Lord, because of a lack of pleasure or delight that you find in them. Nor should you do them only for the delight and pleasure they give you. You should equally do these and others that are distasteful to you, otherwise it is impossible for you to gain constancy and overcome your weakness.

Third Caution

17. The third caution is that a spiritual man must never set his eyes upon that which is pleasing in his exercises and hence become attached to them and perform them for this reason only. Nor can he flee from that which is displeasing in them, but rather he must seek that which is toilsome and distasteful; in this way he bridles his sensual nature. If you do otherwise you will neither lose your self-love, nor win and attain the love of God.

Four Counsels to a Religious for the Attainment of Perfection

IN a few words, your Holy Charity has asked a great deal of me, for which much time and paper would be necessary. As I find myself with neither of these, I will try to summarize and set down only certain points which contain much in a small place and will lead anyone who observes them perfectly to achieve great perfection. Anyone who wants to be a true religious and fulfill the duties of the state which he has vowed to conform to before God and make progress in the virtues and enjoy the consolations and delight of the Holy Spirit will be unable to do this unless he strives with the greatest care to put into practice the four following maxims: resignation, mortification, the practice of virtues and solitude of body and of spirit.

2. In order to observe the first of these, resignation, one must live in the monastery as if no one else lived there. He should never meddle, either in word or in thought, with the things that happen in the community, nor with individuals, nor anything concerning them, be it good or evil, nor with their personal qualities. And even if the world were to end, in order to preserve his tranquility of soul, he must not remark upon them nor meddle with them, but rather should remember Lot's wife who was turned to stone because she turned her head at the cries and the noise made by those who were dying. The religious must observe this very strictly and thus he will free himself from many sins and imperfections, and will preserve his tranquility and quietness of soul, and will make great progress in the sight of God

and in that of men. Great attention should be paid to this, for it is of such importance that many religious, because they have failed to observe it, have not only not profited by their other works of virtue and religion, but have continually fallen away and gone from bad to worse.

3. In order to put into practice the second maxim, mortification, and to make progress in this the religious must truly set this truth in his heart: he has come to the convent only in order to be formed and tried in virtue, and that he is like the stone which must be polished and formed before it can be set in the building. And so he must realize that all who are in the convent are no more than workmen that God has put there solely to form and polish him in regards to mortification. Some are to form him in word, telling him what he would prefer not to hear; others in deed, doing things which he would prefer not to endure; others in character, being tiresome and troublesome to him both in themselves and in their behavior; others in thought, so that he feels or thinks that they neither esteem nor love him. All of these mortifications and annoyances he must endure with inner patience, keeping silence for the love of God and realizing that he entered the religious life for no other reason than that he might thus be formed and made worthy of heaven. For if he did not enter it with that intention, there would be no reason for having entered; rather he should have remained in the world, seeking his own comfort, honor, credit, and ease.

4. This second maxim is absolutely necessary if the religious is to fulfill the duties of his state and find true humility, interior quiet and joy in the Holy Spirit. If he does not put it into practice, nor learn how to be a religious, or even the reason why he entered the reli-

gious life, nor learn to seek Christ, but only seeks himself, he will neither find peace in his soul nor will he fail to sin and often be troubled. For occasions of these failings will never be lacking in the religious life, nor would God want them to be lacking. Since He brings souls into this life in order to prove and purify them, as gold is purified with fire and hammer, it is proper that there is no lack of trials and temptations of men and of devils, nor of the fire of troubles and afflictions. In these things the religious must exercise himself, endeavoring always to bear them with patience, conforming to the will of God, and not in such a way that, instead of approving him in his time of trial, God will have to reprove him for not having been willing to bear the cross of Christ with patience. Many religious, not realizing that they have entered the religious life for this purpose, endure others with difficulty, and will find themselves put to great shame and confusion when they come to their accounting.

5. In order to put the third counsel, the exercise of virtues, into practice, it is necessary for the religious to be constant in practicing the acts of his religious life and in obedience, with no regard to the world, but for God's sake alone. In order that he may do this without being deceived, he should never consider the pleasure or displeasure which he finds in work, in doing it or refraining from it, but consider only that he does it for God's sake. Thus he should do all things, whether pleasurable or distasteful, for the sole purpose of serving God in this way.

6. In order to put this into practice with determination and constancy, and to bring forth the virtues quickly, he should always incline toward that which is difficult rather than that which is easy, toward the rough

rather than the smooth, toward the grievous and distasteful part of his work rather than the delightful and pleasant. He should not select what is only a light cross, for that is an unworthy burden; and the greater the burden, the lighter it is, if borne for God. He must always strive to see that his brothers are preferred to him in all comforts and always put himself in the lowest place with a good will. For this is the way to become great in spirituality, as God tells us in His Gospel: *Qui se humiliat exaltabitur.*

7. To put the fourth counsel, solitude, into practice, the religious must consider all the things of the world as ended, so that, when he is obliged against his will to engage in them, he may have a great detachment toward them as if they did not exist.

8. He should not take any account of things outside, since God has withdrawn him from them and led him to neglect them. He should not do any business himself that he could do by means of a third person, for it is appropriate for him to desire to see no one and to be seen by none. He must carefully consider that if God will exact from any one of the faithful a strict account of any idle word, how much more will He exact an account of every word, on the day of reckoning, from a religious, whose whole life and work are consecrated to God?

9. I do not mean by this that a religious should fail to perform with all necessary and possible care the office which he holds, or anything that is required of him by obedience. He must do this in such a way that no blame can be attached to him, because neither God nor obedience wants this. In order to do this he must be constant in prayer, not abandoning it even when he is exercising his body. Whether he is eating, drinking, speaking,

conversing with persons in the world, or whatever he may be doing, he must always be desiring God and have his heart turned to Him; for this is most necessary for interior solitude, which demands that the soul has no thought that is not directed to God, forgetting all things which belong to this short and miserable life and which pass away. In no way should he seek to know anything except how he may better serve God and keep His ordinances more faithfully.

10. If your Charity observes these four things with care, you will very quickly attain perfection; for they are of such mutual assistance to each other that, if a man is imperfect in one of them, he loses all that he was gaining by making progress in the others.

CONTENTS

Sayings of Light and Love *

I

Interior Mortification

To be silent, with the desire and with the tongue, before this great God is what is most necessary in order to make progress, for the language which He hears best is the silent language of love.

The heavens are stable and not subject to generation, and souls which are of heavenly texture are also stable, and are not subject to the generation of desires or to anything else; for according to their nature they are like God, and are never moved.

Although you perform many actions, you will make no progress in perfection if you do not learn to deny your will and to submit yourself, losing all anxiety about yourself and your own affairs.

If you want devotion to be born in your spirit, and the love of God and desire for Divine things to grow,

*This is the Saint's own description of these maxims.

29

cleanse your soul of every desire, attachment and pretension so that you care nothing for anything. For just as a sick man, when he has rid himself of his illness, is immediately aware of good health and wants to eat, so you will recover your health in God when you cure yourself in this way. Otherwise, no matter how much you do it will profit you nothing.

A soul with the least desire for worldly things has greater unfitness and impurity in its journey to God than if, as long as its rational will rejected them, it were burdened with all the hideous and persistent temptations and works of darkness describable. For the soul in the latter state can approach God with confidence to do the will of His Majesty, who says: "Come to Me, all you who are weary and heavy-laden, and I will give you rest."

Renounce your desires and you will find what your heart desires. How do you know if your desire is according to God?

Since if you fulfill your desire, you will have a double measure of bitterness, do not desire to fulfill it even if you remain in bitterness.

He who knows how to die in all things will have life in all things.

The difficulties of a bird that is caught in the lime are twofold: first it has to free itself and then it must clean itself. The troubles of one who fulfills his desires are twofold: first he must free himself, and then, once free, must purify himself from that which has clung to him.

He who does not allow himself to be carried away by his desires will soar upward with ease in the spirit, even as a bird with many feathers.

A fly that clings to honey hinders itself from flying; the soul that clings to spiritual delight hinders its own liberty and contemplation.

I did not know You, my Lord, because I still desired to know and delight in things.

Consider that your guardian angel does not always move the desire to act, although he always illumines the reason. Therefore do not wait for desire before performing a virtuous deed, since reason and understanding are sufficient.

The desire gives the angel no cause to move it when it is set upon something else.

Consider that the most delicate flower withers and loses its fragrance soonest. Therefore beware of seeking to walk in the way of spiritual delight, for you will not be constant. But choose spiritual vigor for yourself, have no attachments, and you will find delight and peace in abundance. Fruit that is delicious and lasting is found in cold, dry country.

If you desire to attain holy recollection, you will attain it by denying, not by accepting.

In order to attain perfection a man must endeavor to be satisfied with nothing, so that his natural and spiritual concupiscence will be content with emptiness. This is necessary for a man who wants to attain the highest tranquility and peace of spirit; in this way the love of God is almost continually in action in the simple and pure soul.

Since God is inaccessible, do not concern yourself with how much your faculties can comprehend and your senses can perceive or you will be satisfied with less and your soul will lose the swiftness that is necessary for one who wants to attain Him.

The soul that does not shake off anxiety and does not quench desire in its journey toward God is like a man who drags a cart uphill.

Strive to work in detachment and desire others to do so.

Readiness in obedience, joy in suffering, mortification of the sight, the desire to know nothing, silence and hope.

You will subject people and things will serve you without labor on your part, if you forget both them and yourself.

You do not know the blessings with which your soul will be recollected if you have interior detachment from all things and do not set your pleasure in any temporal thing.

The poor man who is naked will be clothed; and the soul that is naked of desires, of willings and not willings will be clothed by God with His purity, desire and will.

If you are detached from that which is without, within, and even the things of God, prosperity will not detain you nor will adversity hinder you.

Another maxim for conquering desire: Have an habitual desire to imitate Christ in all His works, conforming yourself to His life, which you must meditate on in order to imitate it and to behave in all things as He would.

In order that you may be able to do this, it is necessary that every desire or taste be renounced, unless it is purely for the honor and glory of God, and that you remain in emptiness for the love of Him who neither did nor desired to do in this life other than the will of His Father, which He called His meat and drink.

Five evils are caused in the soul by any desire: first, it is made uneasy; second, it is confused; third, it is soiled; fourth, it is weakened; and fifth, it is darkened.

Strive always to choose not that which is easiest, but that which is most difficult; not what is most delightful, but what is most unpleasing; not what gives most pleasure, but what gives no pleasure. Choose not what is restful, but what is most wearisome; not what gives consolation, but what gives no consolation; not what is greatest, but what is least; not what is loftiest and most precious, but what is lowest and most despised; not what is a desire for anything, but what is a desire for nothing; seek not the best things but the worst; and to have detachment, emptiness, and poverty with respect to that which is in the world, for Jesus Christ's sake.

33

II

Exterior Mortification

REMEMBER that your flesh is weak and that nothing belonging to the world can give strength or consolation to your spirit. For that which is born of the world is worldly, and that which is born of the flesh is fleshly; and true spirituality is born of the spirit alone, which is communicated neither through the world nor the flesh.

Do not weary yourself, for you will not enter into spiritual delight and sweetness unless you give yourself to moritifcation of all that you desire.

On the road to life there is very little bustle and business, and it requires mortification of the will rather than much knowledge. He who encumbers himself least with things and pleasures will go farthest along the road.

Let us consider how necessary it is for us to be our own enemies, and to journey to perfection on the road of holy severity. Let us understand that every word we speak, save by command and under obedience, is laid to our account by God.

Let Christ Crucified be sufficient for you; suffer and rest with Him. For this purpose annihilate yourself with respect to all things, both without and within.

Truly a man has conquered all things if the pleasure they bring does not move him to joy and the insipidity they leave behind does not cause him sorrow.

He who complains or murmurs is not perfect, nor is he even a good Christian.

It is better to conquer the tongue than to fast on bread and water.

Do not contradict; and never speak impure words.

The habits of voluntary imperfections which are never completely conquered not only hinder Divine union, but also prevent a soul from approaching perfection. Such imperfections are: the habit of speaking too much; little unconquered attachments, such as for persons, clothes, cells, books, different kinds of food; other conversations; preferences in tasting things; in knowing and hearing; and other similar things.

Crucified inwardly and outwardly with Christ, a man will live in this life with fullness and satisfaction of soul, possessing his soul in patience.

III

Purity of Intention

A good work performed for God's sake, in purity and singleness of heart, in a breast that is pure, makes a kingdom of singleness of heart for him who performs it.

God desires the least degree of purity of conscience more than all the works that you can perform.

One good work, however small it is, that is done in secret with no desire that it be known is more pleasing to God than a thousand that are done with a desire for them to be known by others. He who does such works for God's sake with the purest love not only does not care if others see him, but does not care if God sees him. Such a man, even though God were never to know it, would not cease to do Him the same service with the same joy and purity of love.

Take no heed of creatures if you wish to keep the image of God clearly and simply in your soul; empty your spirit of them and withdraw far from them. Then you will walk in the Divine light, for God is not like creatures.

The spirit that is truly pure does not advert to exterior things, or to human regard, but inwardly, alone and withdrawn from all forms, and in delightful tranquility, it communes with God, for knowledge is in Divine silence.

My spirit has dried up in me because it forgets to feed on You.

If you purify your soul of strange possessions and desires, you will understand the things of the spirit; and if you deny your desire concerning them, you will enjoy the truth that is in them, understanding what is certain in them.

Do not think that pleasing God lies so much in performing numerous good works as in performing them with a good will, without attachment and respect for persons.

An intimate desire that God may grant you that which His Majesty knows you lack for His honor.

Have a loving attentiveness to God, with no desire to feel or understand anything in particular concerning Him.

There are souls that wallow in the mire even as animals wallow in it, and others that soar like birds who purify and cleanse themselves in the air.

Hair that is combed frequently is untangled, and will not be difficult to comb as often as one wants; the soul that frequently examines its thoughts, words and deeds, which are like hair, and that does all things for love of God, will find that its hair is quite free of entanglement. Then the Spouse will look upon the neck of the Bride, and will be captivated, and wounded by one of her eyes, that is, by the purity of intention with which she performs all her acts. We begin to comb our hair from the crown of the head if we want to keep it untangled; so all our works must begin from the crown, that is, from the love of God, if we wish to be pure and unentangled.

Rid yourself of what is human in order to seek God. A man uses a light in his outer life so that he will not fall, but light acts in the opposite way in the things of God. Therefore it is better not to see and in this way the soul has more security.

Rest, put your anxieties far from you, do not care at all for what comes, and you will serve God as He wills and find happiness in Him.

IV

Spiritual Direction

HE who desires to be alone, without the support of a master and guide will be like a tree that is alone in the field and has no owner. No matter how much fruit it bears, passers-by will pick it all and it will not mature.

The tree that is cultivated and kept with the help of its owner gives the fruit that is expected of it at the right season.

The soul that is alone and without a guide and has virtue is like a burning coal that is alone. It will grow colder rather than hotter.

He who falls alone remains on the ground alone and holds his soul of small account, since he trusts it to himself alone.

If you do not fear to fall alone, how do you presume to rise alone? See how much more can be done by two together than by one alone!

He who falls heavily laden will have difficulty in rising with his load.

He who falls and is blind will not, in his blindness rise up alone; and if he does, he will journey where it is not fitting.

V

Diligence

HE who loses an opportunity is like one who lets a bird fly out of his hand, for he will not regain it.

How do you presume to take your ease so fearlessly since you must appear before God to give an account of the least of your words and thoughts?

Behold how many are called and how few are chosen. Realize that if you have no care for yourself, your damnation is more certain than your changing, especially as the way that leads to eternal life is narrow.

He who works lukewarmly is near to falling.

Since when your hour of reckoning comes it will grieve you that you have not used this time in the service of God, why do you not order and use it now as you would wish to have if you were dying?

VI

Prudence

WISDOM enters through love, silence and mortification; great wisdom is to be able to keep silence, and to not look at the words, deeds, or lives of others.

Accept your reason; do what it counsels you on the road to God. This will be of greater worth to you in respect to God than all the works you do without this counsel and all the spiritual delights you seek.

Blessed is he who puts aside his pleasure and inclination and regards things according to reason and justice in order to perform them.

For what cannot be sensed, what you do not sense, for what can be sensed, sensation; and for the Spirit of God, thought.

He who acts according to reason is like one who eats substantial food, and he who is moved by the desire of his will is like one who eats insipid fruit.

Do not meddle in the affairs of others, nor even allow them to pass through your memory, for perhaps you will be unable to fulfill your task.

Do not rejoice in temporal prosperity because you do not know with certainty that it assures you eternal life.

Man does not know how to rejoice properly or to grieve properly, for he does not understand the distance there is between good and evil.

Speak little and do not meddle in things when you have not been consulted.

Never allow yourself to pour out your heart, even though only for a moment.

VII

Obedience

GOD desires more the least degree of obedience and submission from you than all those services you think to do Him.

The venerable and blessed Father John of the Cross was once asked how a man went into ecstasy. "By renouncing his own will," he replied, "and doing the will of God. For ecstasy is only the going out of a soul from itself and being caught up in God, and this is what happens to the soul that is obedient. That is that it goes out of itself and its own desires, and thus lightened, becomes immersed in God!"

To be prepared to lose and see all others win belongs to valiant souls, to generous and liberal hearts. One of the qualities of such souls is that they will give rather than receive even until they come to give themselves, for they consider the possession of themselves to be a great burden, and prefer to be possessed by others and withdrawn from themselves, for we belong to that infinite Good rather than to ourselves.

VIII

Suffering

THE purest suffering bears and carries in its train the purest understanding.

My Beloved, all that is rough and toilsome I desire for myself, and all that is sweet and delightful I desire for You.

It is better to be heavy burdened and near one who is strong than relieved of one's load and near one who is weak. When you are heavy burdened you are near God Who is your Strength, and is with those in trouble. When you are relieved, you are near only yourself, who is your own weakness. For the virtue and strength of the soul grows and is confirmed by trials of patience.

God esteems more in you an inclination toward aridity and suffering for love of Him than all the consolations, spiritual visions, and meditations that you may have.

God is more pleased by the soul that in aridity and trial submits to that which is reason than the soul which fails to do this but receives consolations from everything that it does.

In tribulation, draw near to God with confidence and you will be strengthened, illumined and instructed.

Rejoice habitually in God Who is your Salvation; realize that it is good to suffer in any way for Him Who is good.

Love trials greatly and hold them at small account if you wish to attain the favor of the Spouse, Who did not hesitate to die for you.

Have fortitude against all things that tempt you to

what is not God; be a lover of the Passion of Christ.

We must measure our trials by ourselves and not ourselves by our trials.

Who does not seek the Cross of Christ does not seek the glory of Christ.

If a soul becomes more patient in suffering and readier to endure lack of consolations, this is a sign that it is making progress in virtue.

It is better to suffer for God's sake than to work miracles.

Be strong in your heart against all things that move you to that which is not God, and for Christ's sake love suffering.

Do not become sorrowful suddenly because of the adversities that are in the world since you do not know the blessings they bring with them, being ordained in the judgments of God for the lasting joy of the elect.

IX

Humility

GOD does not conceive love for the soul by considering its greatness, but by considering the greatness of its humility.

What you seek and most desire you will not find by your way, not by lofty contemplation, but rather by deep humility and submissiveness of heart.

Do not rejoice vainly, for you do not know how many sins you have committed nor how you stand with God; but fear, yet have confidence.

Think constantly of eternal life, and of the truth that they who are lowliest, poorest, and counted as least will have the greatest dominion and glory in God.

Allow yourself to be taught; allow yourself to be commanded; allow yourself to be brought into submission and despised; and you will be perfect.

If you desire glory and do not wish to appear stupid and foolish, put away all the things that are not yours, and you will have glory for what remains. But in truth, if you put away all things that are not yours, you will be changed into nothing, for you must glory in nothing if you do not wish to fall into vanity. But let us turn now especially to the gifts of those graces which make men full of grace and pleasing in the eyes of God. It is certain that you should not glory in those gifts since you do not know yet if you have them.

Love to be unknown both by yourself and others. Never look at the good or evil things of others.

Great damage and harm are done to the secrecy of the conscience whenever its fruits are manifested to men, for in such a case, the soul receives its reward in the fruits of transitory fame.

Do not excuse yourself nor refuse to be corrected by

all; listen to every reproof with a serene countenance; think that God utters it.

If at times some good word is spoken of you, count it as the mercy of God, for you deserve none.

Be silent concerning what God may give you and remember the saying of the Bride: "My secret for myself."

He who trusts to himself is worse than the devil.

He is humble who hides himself in his own nothingness and knows how to cast himself upon God.

Try to speak against yourself and to desire that all may do so.

Perfection does not lie in the virtues which the soul knows itself to have; it consists in those which Our Lord sees in the soul. This is a closed book. Therefore the soul has no excuse for presumption, but must humble itself to the ground with respect to its virtues.

X

Presence of God

TAKE God for your Spouse, for a Friend with Whom you walk continually, and you will not sin and will learn to love; and the things that are needful will come about prosperously for you.

In joys and pleasures draw immediately near to God with fear and truth, and you will neither be deceived nor turned to vanity.

Enter into your heart and labor in the presence of the Spouse, Who is always present and loves you well.

There are three signs of interior recollection: first, if the soul has no pleasure in transitory things; second, if it has pleasure in solitude and silence and pays attention to all that leads to greater perfection; third, if the things which once helped it (such as considerations, meditations and acts) now hinder it and the soul has no other support in prayer except faith, hope and charity.

The soul that is united with God is feared by the devil as though it were God Himself.

Strictly restrain your tongue, fix your affection habitually on God, and the Divine Spirit will give it great fervor. Read this often.

The farther you withdraw yourself from earthly things, the nearer you approach heavenly things and the more you find in God.

Strive always to have God present in you and keep within yourself the purity that God teaches.

Live in this world as though there were none in it but God and your soul, so that your heart may be detained by nothing that is human.

How sweet will Your presence be to me, You Who are

46

the highest Good. I will approach You with silence and uncover my feet before you that you may be pleased to unite me to You in marriage. I will not take my rest until I have fruition of Yourself in Your arms. And now I entreat You, Lord, not to forsake me at any time in my recollection since I am a spendthrift of my soul.

XI

Prayer

SEEK in reading and you will find in meditation; knock in prayer and it will be opened to you in contemplation.

Behold that infinite knowledge and that hidden secret. What peace, love, and silence are in the Divine Bosom! How great a science is that which God teaches there: that is, the silence of what we call anagogical acts, which so greatly enkindle the heart.

It is a great evil to have an eye to the good things of God rather than to God Himself, to prayer and detachment.

Be unwilling to admit into your soul things which have in themselves no spiritual substance, so that they do not make you lose your desire for devotion and recollection.

One word spoke the Father, which Word was His Son, and this Word He speaks always in eternal silence, and in silence it must be heard by the soul.

47

The whole world is not worthy of a man's thought, for it is the work of God alone, and whatever thought of ours is not centered on God is stolen from Him.

The faculties and senses must not be employed wholly upon things, but only insofar as is unavoidable. With this exception all must be left free for God.

Do not look at the imperfections of others; keep silence and have continual converse with God. These three will uproot great imperfection from the soul and will make it the mistress of great virtues.

There are five characteristics of the solitary bird. First, it soars as high as possible. Second, it can endure no companionship, even of its own kind. Third, it has its beak in the air. Fourth, it has no definite color. Fifth, it sings sweetly. These characteristics will belong to the contemplative soul. It must soar above transitory things acting as if they did not exist. It must be so fond of solitude and silence that it cannot endure the companionship of another creature. Its beak must be in the atmosphere of the Holy Spirit, that is, it must respond to His inspirations, in order that it may become more worthy of His companionship. It must have no definite color, that is, it must not desire to do any definite thing except that which is the will of God. It must sing sweetly in the contemplation and love of its Spouse.

He who flees from prayer flees from all that is good.

XII

Conformity to the Divine Will

WHAT good is it if you give one thing to God when He asks you for another? Consider what will please God and do it; in this way you will better satisfy your heart than with that toward which you incline.

O Lord, my God! Whoever seeks You with simple and pure love will not fail to find You, Who are dear to his desire and will, because You show Yourself first of all and go out to meet those who desire You.

Renounce your desires and you will find what your heart desires. How do you know if your desire is according to God?

Though the road is plain and easy for men of good will, he who journeys on it will not go far and will find many trials on the way unless he has good feet and courage and the perseverance that comes from courage.

If I go, my God, where You go, it will be this way for me as I desire for Your Sake.

A soul united with God is feared by the devil as though it were God Himself. The soul that desires God to surrender Himself wholly to it must surrender itself to Him wholly and leave nothing for itself.

If you wish to be perfect, sell your will and give it to the poor in spirit; come to Christ in meekness and humility and follow Him to Calvary and the grave.

XIII

Peace

FIND spiritual tranquility in a loving attentiveness to God, and if it is necessary to speak, let it be with the same tranquility and peace.

Let everything be changed, and willingly, Lord God, so that we may find rest in You.

Withdraw from evil, work good and seek peace.

It is not God's will that the soul allow anything to trouble it or suffer trials; if it suffers in the adversities of the world, this comes from a weakness of its virtue. For the soul of a perfect man rejoices in that which is affliction in an imperfect soul.

Realize that God reigns only in the disinterested and peaceful soul.

If you desire to find peace and contentment for your soul, and to truly serve God, do not be content with what you have left behind, for perhaps you will still have as many impediments as before, or even more than before. But leave all these other things that are still before you and withdraw yourself to the one thing alone which brings everything with it: that is, to holy solitude, together with prayer and with holy and divine reading and remain there in forgetfulness of all things. For if these things are not required of you by obligation, you will be more pleasing to God by being able to keep yourself, and make yourself; more perfect than by gaining all other things at once. For what will it profit a man if he gains the whole world and loses his soul?

Do not feed your spirit on anything but God. Cast out concern for all things and have peace and recollection in your heart.

Strive to keep your heart in peace, and do not let anything that happens in this world make you uneasy, for consider that it must all come to an end.

XIV

Love of Neighbor

YOU, Lord, return gladly and lovingly to exalt him who offends You, and I do not return to exalt and honor him who angers me.

Do not think that, because another man does not shine with the virtues which you perceive, he will not be precious in God's sight, for reasons you do not perceive.

He is meek who knows how to suffer his neighbor and to suffer his own self.

Never hear the weaknesses of others, and then, if anyone complains to you of another, you will be able to tell him humbly to say nothing of it to you.

Do not complain of anyone, ask nothing, or, if it is necessary for you to ask, let it be with few words.

Do not refuse work, even though it appears to you that you cannot do it. Let all find compassion in you.

Let your speech be such that no one can be offended by it, and speak of things about which you are not bothered if everyone knows of them.

Deny nothing that you have, even if you have need of it.

He who does not love his neighbor, abhors God.

Habitual confidence in God, esteeming in oneself and in others what God most esteems, that is, spiritual blessings.

XV

Divine Love

O sweetest love of God that is so little known! He who has found the veins of this mine has found rest.

One single thought of a man is of greater worth than the whole world; therefore God alone is worthy of him.

The soul in the union of love has not even the first movements of sin.

The soul enkindled with love is a soul that is gentle, meek, humble and patient.

More profit can be obtained from the good things of

God in one hour than from our own good things in a whole lifetime.

Strictly restrain your tongue and your thoughts; keep your affection habitually fixed on God and He will grant your spirit divine fervor.

He who is ashamed to confess Me before men, says the Lord, I will also be ashamed to confess before My Father.

The soul that is hard becomes harder through love of itself. If in Your love, O good Jesus, You do not soften the soul, it will persist forever in its natural hardness.

The tried friends of God very rarely fail God, because they are above all that they can lack.

Never take a man as an example for what you must do, however holy he is, or else the devil will set his imperfections before you. But imitate Christ Who is the sum of perfection and holiness, and you will never go astray.

Do not eat of the forbidden fruit which belongs to this present life, since blessed are they who hunger and thirst after righteousness, for they will be filled. What God seeks to do is to make us gods by participation, as He is God by nature, just as fire converts all things into fire.

He who works for God with pure love does not care whether or not men know it, but also does not do things in order that God knows it. Such a one would not cease to do these same services and with the same gladness and love even if it were never known.

O powerful Lord, if a spark of Your empire of righteousness has so great an effect upon a prince who is mortal and who governs and moves people, what effect will Your omnipotent righteousness have upon the righteous man and the sinner?

All the goodness that we have is lent to us and God considers it His own work. God and His work is God.

Love does not consist in feeling great things, but in having great detachment and in suffering for the Beloved.

All for Me and nothing for you.

All for You and nothing for me.

Twelve means for arriving at the highest perfection are: love of God, love of neighbor, obedience, chastity, poverty, attendance at choir, penance, humility, mortification, prayer, silence, peace.

Do not trouble yourself, either a little or a lot, as to who is against you and who is with you. Strive always to please your God. Pray to Him that His will may be done in you. Love Him greatly, for you owe Him this.

The soul that walks in love does not weary nor is it wearied.

The Lord has always revealed the treasures of His

wisdom and His spirit to mortals; but now that wickedness is revealing its face more and more clearly, He reveals them in large measure.

My God and Lord, You are no stranger to him who does not make himself a stranger to You. How can they say that You absent Yourself?

Oh what blessings we will enjoy with the sight of the Most Holy Trinity!

A Prayer of the Soul Enkindled with Love

LORD, God, my Beloved! If you still remember my sins and do not do what I am always beseeching You to, do Your will concerning them, my God, for it is this that I most desire; exercise Your goodness and mercy and You will be known in them. If You wait for my works in order to grant me my prayer, grant them to me and work them in me and impose on me the penalties You will accept, and let Your will be done. If You are not waiting for my works, what are You waiting for, my most merciful Lord? Why do You tarry? For if it is grace and mercy which I entreat of You in Your Son, take my small thing, since You desire it, and grant me this good thing, since You also desire it.

Who can free himself from limitations and base ways of acting, if You do not raise him up to Yourself, my God, in purity of love?

How will a man who is engendered and nurtured in baseness rise up to You, if You, O Lord, do not raise him up with the hand with which You made him.

You will not take from me, my God, that which You gave me in Your only Son Jesus Christ, in Whom You gave me all that I desire. Therefore I will rejoice that You will not tarry if I wait for You.

With what procrastinations do you wait, since even now you cannot love God in your heart?

The heavens are mine, and the earth is mine; the people are mine; the righteous are mine; the sinners are mine; the angels are mine; and the Mother of God and all things are mine; God Himself is mine and for me, for Christ is mine and all for me. What, then, do you ask for and seek, my soul? Yours is all this, and it is all for you.

Do not consider yourself as nothing, nor pay attention to the crumbs which fall from your Father's table. Leave them and glory in your glory. Hide yourself in this and rejoice and you will have the desires of your heart.

Poems

I

Upon a darksome night,
Kindling with love in flame of yearning keen
—O moment of delight!—
I went, by all unseen,
New-hush'd to rest the house where I had been.

Safe sped I through that night,
By the secret stair, disguised and unseen,
—O moment of delight!—
Wrapt in that night serene,
New-hush'd to rest the house where I had been.

O happy night and blest!
Secretly speeding, screen'd from mortal gaze,
Unseeing, on I prest,
Lit by no earthly rays,
Nay, only by heart's inmost fire ablaze.

'Twas that light guided me,
More surely than the noonday's brightest glare,
To the place where none would be
Save one that waited there—
Well knew I whom or ere I forth did fare.

O night that led'st me thus!
O night more winsome than the rising sun!
O night that madest us,
Lover and lov'd, as one,
Lover transform'd in lov'd, love's journey done!

Upon my flowering breast,
His only, as no man but he might prove,
There, slumbering, did he rest,
'Neath my caressing love,
Fann'd by the cedars swaying high above.

When from the turret's height,
Scattering his locks, the breezes play'd around,
With touch serene and light
He dealt me love's sweet wound,
And with the joyful pain thereof I swoon'd.

Forgetful, rapt, I lay,
My face reclining on my lov'd one fair.
All things for me that day
Ceas'd, as I slumber'd there,
Amid the lilies drowning all my care.

II

A shepherd-boy his grief is brooding o'er
Alone, uncomforted, disconsolate.
His thought is fix'd upon his heart's true mate;
His breast with love is stricken very sore.

He weeps not for some love-wound giv'n of yore,
For no such thing could pain and grieve him so,
E'en though it overcharg'd his heart with woe:
He weeps because she thinks of him no more.

And so, because she thinks of him no more
—That shepherd-maid of his, so fair to see—
He lets his alien foes treat cruelly
The breast that love has stricken very sore.

'Woe,' cries the shepherd-boy, 'Woe be in store
For him that's come betwixt my love and me,
So that she wishes not to know or see
This breast that love has stricken very sore.'

Then climbs he slowly, when much time is o'er,
Into a tree, with fair arms wide outspread.
And, clinging to that tree, forthwith is dead,
For lo! his breast was stricken very sore.

How well I know the fount that freely flows
    Although 'tis night!

The eternal fount its source has never show'd.
But well I know wherein is its abode,
    Although 'tis night!

Its origin I know not—it has none:
All other origins are here begun,
    Although 'tis night!

I know that naught beside can be so fair,
That heav'ns and earth drink deep refreshment
  there,
    Although 'tis night!

Well know I that its depths can no man plumb
Nor, fording it, across it hope to come,
    Although 'tis night!

Never was fount so clear, undimm'd and bright:
From it alone, I know, proceeds all light,
    Although 'tis night!

Rich are its streams and full—this know I well;
They water nations, heav'ns and depths of hell,
    Although 'tis night!

Yea, more I know: the stream that hence proceeds,
Omnipotent, suffices for all needs,
    Although 'tis night!

From fount and stream another stream forth
  flows,
And this, I know, in nothing yields to those,
    Although 'tis night!

The eternal fount is hidden in living bread,
That we with life eternal may be fed,
    Although 'tis night!

Call'd to this living fount, we creatures still
Darkly may feed hereon and take our fill,
    Although 'tis night!

This living fount which is so dear to me
Is in the bread of life, which now I see,
    Although 'tis night!

IV

Far away in the beginning
Dwelt the Word in God most High
And in God His bliss eternal
Had He everlastingly.

That same Word was God Almighty,
And Beginning was His name,
For He dwelt in the beginning,
Out of no beginning came.

He Himself was that beginning
Wherefore He Himself had none.
He that sprang from that beginning
Was the Word, called also Son.

Everpast has God conceived Him,
And conceives Him evermore,
Gives Him ever of His substance
Ever shares it as of yore.

Thus His glory in the Father
Is the glory of the Son:
All His glory had the Father
In His best Belovèd One.

As Belovèd dwells in Lover
Each in other did reside,

And that same love that unites Them
Did in both of Them abide;

Each was equal to the Other
And in worth ranked equally.
Thus there were in that tri-union
One Belovèd, Persons three.

One the love that did unite Them,
One the Lover in all Three:
Lover that is the Belovèd,
In Whom each dwelt equally.

For the Being of three Persons
They possess'd the Same Each One,
Each One loving both the Others
Since They had it as Their own.

This same Being is each Person:
Naught but this conjoin'd them well
In a tie so strange and wondrous
That its nature none can tell.

Infinite and everlasting
Was the love that bound Them so.
One alone this love that bound Them
Which as Essence we may know,
And the more this love had oneness,
More the love that thence did grow.

V

When the interval of waiting
For His birth its course had run,
Straight from out His bridal chamber
Came the Bridegroom, God the Son.

Once on earth, with arms extended
He embrac'd His heavenly Bride,
And the gracious Mother laid Him
In the manger, at her side.

All around that helpless baby
Animals were standing by;
Men sang songs of glad rejoicing;
Angels join'd their songs on high,

Celebrating the betrothal
'Twixt the Bridegroom and the Bride,
While the Almighty, in the manger,
As an infant, wept and cried.

So the Bride those tears as jewels
Brought to the betrothal-rite,
And the Maid was lost in wonder
As she saw so rare a sight.

Man was full of joy and gladness;
God was shedding tears as man.
Ne'er was such a strange mutation
Since the ages first began.

Compendium of Perfection

Forgetfulness of things created,
Remembrance of the Creator,
Attention to that which is within,
And continual love for the Beloved.

LETTERS

To the Discalced Carmelite Nuns of Beas

Gives the Discalced nuns admirable instruction concerning emptiness and detachment from creatures.

Jesus be in your souls, daughters. Are you thinking that, since you see me so silent, I have lost sight of you, and cease from considering how with great ease you may become holy, and how, with great delight and under sure protection, you may go rejoicing in the beloved Spouse? Well, I shall come to you and you will see that I have not been forgetting you, and we shall see what wealth you have gained in pure love and in the paths of eternal life and what excellent progress you are making in Christ, Whose brides are His delight and crown: and a crown deserves not merely to be sent rolling along the floor, but to be taken by the angels and seraphim in their hands and set with reverence and esteem on the head of their Lord.

When the heart is occupied with mean things, the crown rolls along the floor, and each of these mean things gives it, as it were, one kick further. But when man attains, as David says, to loftiness of heart, then God is magnified with the crown of that lofty heart of His bride, with which they crown Him in the day of the joy of His heart, in which He has His delights when He is with the sons of men. These waters of interior delights do not have their source in the earth: the mouth of desire must be opened toward Heaven, and must be empty of anything else that might fill it, so that in this way the mouth of desire, neither clogged nor closed by the taste of anything else, may be completely empty and wide open toward Him Who says: "Open your mouth wide and I will fill it for you."

He, then, who seeks pleasure in anything else does not keep himself empty so that God may fill him with His ineffable joy, and in the State in which he goes to God, he goes from Him, for his hands are encumbered and he cannot take what God gives him. May God deliver us from such evil encumbrances, which impede such sweet and delectable freedom.

Serve God, my beloved daughters in Christ, following His footsteps of mortification in all patience, in all silence and with all desire to suffer. Become the executioners of your own pleasures, mortifying yourselves if perhaps there is still anything left in you that has yet to die and that impedes the interior resurrection of the spirit. May that spirit dwell in your souls! Amen.

From Málaga.

Your servant,
Fray John of the Cross

November 18, 1586.

To the Discalced Carmelite Nuns of Beas
[or Granada]

New spiritual instructions for the nuns. What the soul ordinarily needs is not to write and speak but to be silent and act. The best means of preserving one's spirituality is to suffer. Solitude and recollection in God.

Jesus, Mary, Joseph be in your souls, my daughters in Christ. Your letter comforted me greatly: may Our Lord reward you for it! My not having written has not been for lack of willingness, for truly I desire your great good, but because it seems to me that enough has already been said and written for the accomplishment of what is needful; and that what is lacking (if anything is lacking) is not writing or speaking, for of this there is generally too much, but silence and work. And, apart from this, speaking is a distraction, whereas silence and work bring to the spirit recollection and strength. And therefore, when a person once understands what has been said to him for his profit, he needs neither to hear nor to say more, but rather to practice what has been said to him silently and carefully, in humility and charity and self-contempt, and not to go away and seek new things, which serve only to satisfy the appetite in external matters (and even here are unable to satisfy it) and leave the spirit weak and empty, with no interior virtue. Hence such a one profits neither at the beginning nor at the end. He is as one that eats again before he has digested his last meal, who, because his natural heat is divided between both meals, has no strength to convert this food into substance, and becomes indisposed.

It is very necessary, my daughters, to be able to withdraw the spirit from the devil and from sensuality, for otherwise, without knowing it, we shall find our-

71

selves completely failing to make progress and very far removed from the virtues of Christ, and afterwards we shall awaken, and find our work and labor turned inside out. Thinking that our lamp was burning, we shall find it apparently extinguished, for when we blew upon it, and tried to fan its flame, we may rather have put it out. I say, then, that, if this is not to happen, and in order to preserve our spirituality (as I have said) there is no other way than to suffer and work and be silent, and to close the senses by the practice of solitude and the inclination to solitude, and forgetfulness of all creatures and all happenings, even if the world ends. Never, for good or for evil, fail to quiet your hearts with tender love, in order that you may suffer in all things that present themselves. For perfection is of such great moment, and spiritual delight is of so rich a price—may God grant that all this may suffice; for it is impossible to continue to make progress except by working and suffering virtuously, and being completely enwrapped in silence.

I have understood, daughters, that the soul which is easily inclined to talk and converse is but very little inclined towards God; for, when it is inclined toward God, it is at once, as it were, forcibly drawn within itself, that it may be silent and shun all conversation, for God would have the soul enjoy Him more than it enjoys any creature, however excellent and suitable such a creature may be.

I commend myself to the prayers of your Charities; and be certain that, small as my charity is, it is so completely centered in you that I never forget those to whom I owe so much in the Lord. May He be with us all. Amen.

From Granada, on the 22nd of November, 1587.

Fray John of the Cross

The greatest necessity we have is to be silent before this great God with the desire and with the tongue, for the language which He alone hears is the language of silent love.

(Superscription): To Ana de Jesús and the other Discalced Carmelite sisters of the Convent of Granada.

To M. Leonor Bautista, Beas

Commiserates with her on her trials and counsels her to bear them with pleasure, for God's sake.

Jesus be in your Reverence. Do not think, daughter in Christ, that I have ceased to grieve for you in your trials or for those that share them with you; yet, when I remember that God has called you to lead an apostolic life, which is a life of contempt, and is leading you by that road, I am comforted. Briefly, God desires that the religious shall live the religious life in such a way that he shall have done with everything, and everything shall be as nothing to him. For He Himself desires to be the only wealth of the soul and its comfort and its delectable glory. God has granted you a great favor, for now, forgetting all things, your Reverence will be able to rejoice in God alone, and for love of God will care nothing as to what they do with you, since you belong not to yourself but to God.

Let me know if your departure for Madrid is certain, and if the Mother Prioress is coming, and commend me greatly to my daughters Magdalena and Ana, and to them all, for I have no opportunity to write to them.

From Granada, on the 8th of February, (15)88.

Fray John of the Cross

To P. Ambrosio Mariano De San Benito, Prior of Madrid

Changes of convent by certain religious. The Prior and Sub-prior must get on well together. No one should interfere with the novices.

Jesus be in your Reverence. The need for religious, as your Reverence knows, is very great, on account of the large number of existing foundations. Therefore your Reverence must have patience until Fray Miguel leaves you to await the Father Provincial at Pastrana, for he has then to go and complete the foundation of that convent at Molina. The Fathers also thought it would be well to give your Reverence a sub-prior; and so they have given you Fray Ángel, as they think he will get on well with his prior, which is the most necessary thing in a convent. Will your Reverence then give to each of these his letters patent? It will also be well if your Reverence loses no opportunity of seeing that no one, whether a priest or not, meddles with the novices in his dealings with them; for, as your Reverence knows, there is nothing more harmful than to pass through many hands and for others to go about interfering with the novices. It is right to help and relieve Fray Ángel, since he has so many novices, and also to give him the authority which belongs to a sub-prior, as we have done, so that he may be the more respected in the house. As to Fray Miguel, it seems that there is no great need for him to be here just now, and that he will be able to serve the Order better elsewhere. With regard to Father Gracián, nothing new has happened, except that Fray Antonio is now here.

From Segovia, November 9, (15)88.

Fray John of the Cross

To Dona Juana De Pedraza, Granada

The Saint acknowledges the letters which his spiritual daughter, Doña Ana, has written him. Spiritual counsels: detachment from everything and blind obedience to the spiritual director. It is fitting that we should never be without our cross. He begs her not to write such tiny letters.

Jesus be in your soul. A few days ago I wrote to you by way of Fray Juan, replying to this your last letter, which, as was to be expected, was greatly valued. In that letter I said that, as far as I can see, I have received all your letters, and have sympathized with your griefs and troubles and times of loneliness, which, even when you have said nothing about them, have always cried out to me to such an extent that even with your pen you could not have said more. All these things are rappings and knockings upon the soul, calling it to greater love, and causing more prayer and sighings of the spirit of God, that He may fulfill that for which the soul begs for His sake. I told you that there was no cause to enter that . . . . , but that you must do what you are commanded, and, if you are hindered from doing this, be obedient and tell me about it, and God will provide what is best. God takes care of the affairs of those who love Him truly without their being anxious concerning them.

In matters pertaining to the soul, it is best for you, so as to be on the safe side, to have attachment to nothing and desire for nothing, and to have true and complete attachment and desire for him who is your proper guide, for to do otherwise would be not to desire a guide. And when one guide suffices, and you have one who suits you, all others are either superfluous or harmful. Let your soul cling to nothing; and, if you fail not to pray,

God will take care of your affairs, for they belong to no other master than God, nor can they do so. This I find to be true of myself, for, the more things are mine, the more I have my heart and soul in them and the more anxious I am about them; for he that loves becomes one with the object of his love, as does God with him that loves Him. Hence one cannot forget this without forgetting one's own soul; and for the object of one's love one indeed forgets one's own soul, for one lives more in the object of one's love than in oneself.

O great God of love, and Lord, how much of Your own riches have You not given to him who loves nothing and takes pleasure in nothing except You, since You give Yourself to him and make him one with Yourself in love! In this You cause him to love and have pleasure in what the soul most desires in You and which brings it the greatest profit. For we must not be without our cross, even as our Beloved had His cross until He died the death of love. He orders our sufferings in the love of that which we most need, so that we may make greater sacrifices and be of greater worth. But it is all short, for it continues only until the knife is raised, and then Isaac remains alive, with the promise that his children shall be multiplied.

Patience is necessary, my daughter, in this poverty, for patience enables us to leave our country, and to enter into life to have full fruition of it all, which is . . . of life.

Now I do not know when I shall go. I am well, although my soul lags far behind. Commend me to God and give the letters to Fray Juan, or to the nuns, more often, whenever you can; it would be better if they were not so tiny.

From Segovia, on January 28, 1589.

Fray John of the Cross

To a Carmelite Nun who Suffered from Scruples

He gives her prudent and wise rules for behavior when attacked by scruples, so that they may do no harm to her soul.

Jesus, Mary. In these days be employed inwardly in desiring the coming of the Holy Spirit, and both during the festival and afterwards continue in His presence, and let your care and esteem for this be such that nothing else attracts you, nor consider anything else, whether it be trouble or any other disturbing memories; and during the whole of this period, even if there are omissions in the house, pass them over for the love of the Holy Spirit, and for the sake of what is necessary for the peace and quiet of the soul in which He loves to dwell.

If you can put an end to your scruples, I think it would be better for your quietness if you were not to confess during these days. When you do confess, let it be in this manner: with regard to advertences and thoughts, whether they have respect to judgments or whether to unruly representations of objects or any other movements that come to you without the desire and collaboration of your soul, and without your desiring to pay attention to them, do not confess these or take any notice of them or be anxious about them, for it is better to forget them, although they trouble your soul the more; at most you might describe in general terms the omission or remissness that you may perhaps have noted with respect to the purity and perfection which you should have in the interior faculties—memory, understanding and will. With respect to words, confess any excess and imprudence that you may have committed as regards speaking truly and uprightly, and out of necessity and with purity of intention. With regard to actions, confess the way in which you may have diverged from the path to your true and only goal, which you should follow without respect of persons—namely, God alone.

And, if you confess in this way, you may rest content, without confessing any of these other things in particular, however much interior conflict it may bring you. You will communicate during this festival, as well as at your usual times.

When anything disagreeable or displeasing happens to you, remember Christ crucified and be silent.

Live in faith and hope, even if it is in darkness, for in this darkness God protects the soul. Cast your care upon God, for you are His and He will not forget you. Do not think that He is leaving you alone, for that would be to wrong Him.

Read, pray, rejoice in God, your Good and your Health, and may He give you His good things and preserve you wholly, even to the day of eternity. Amen. Amen.

Fray John of the Cross